Enjoy and "taste" Aussie land and people! Love Juliee

Mainly For Mums

By Margaret Lemmon

To Jill Benson
my doctor and my
very best friend

ISBN: 1 86476 007 9

Copyright © Axiom Publishing
First Edition 1998
Second Printing 1999
Third Printing 2000

Axiom
Australia

Contents

The Beginning

I've collected a few of my poems,
That I've written over the years.
Some are funny, Some are naughty,
Some may bring a tear.
But I hope that you will like them,
As you read my little book.
And maybe there will be some of you
Who'll take a second look
At certain ones I've written,
And Identify with them,
And say, "That's exactly how it is."
Or, "I had that feeling THEN."

Show Her You Care

A Mother is a person,
Quite apart from all the rest.
She gives her never ending love,
She gives her very best.
She helps you, guides you, comforts you,
Whenever you feel blue,
She's always there to lend a hand,
In everything you do.
She listens to your problems,
And all your joys she shares,
And any time you need a friend,
You'll find she's always there.
So don't take her for granted,
let her know how much you care,
'Cause you'll never know her value,
Till you see her empty chair.

Who Would Be a Mother?

So many times when we were young,
I'd hear my Mother say,
"Who would be a Mother?"
Why did she speak that way?

I know that sometimes we were sick,
Or we wouldn't go to school,
But they were only Little things,
That shouldn't worry her at all.

We'd leave our bedrooms in a mess,
We'd stay out late at night,
But I don't know why she worried,
We knew we were all right.

We wouldn't eat our vegies,
'Cause we liked our pies and buns,
And when she caught us smoking,
She went on about our lungs.

There were so many Little things,
That made her make a fuss,
And I couldn't understand it,
'Cause they never worried us.

Well now that I am married,
And children I've got three,
Those words my Mother used to say,
Keep coming back to me.

That phrase she would so often use,
When to her feelings she'd give vent,
God, "Who would be a Mother?"
Now I know Just What she meant.

The Cost of Living

How much for that latest creation
That I saw in the shops today,
To make a big impression,
And have others look my way?

How much for those latest gadgets for my kitchen,
And that furniture too,
To make all my neighbours envy me,
Like other people do?

How much for a life of luxury,
Away from the kitchen sink?
I ask myself all these questions,
And I begin to think.

How much would it cost to go on a cruise,
From life's worries to get away?
BUT, How much would it cost to go to the park,
And watch the children play?

How much would it cost to see the bright lights?
BUT, How much are the stars above?
How much if I give that expensive gift?
BUT, How much if instead I give Love?

How much would it cost if I walk away?
BUT, How much if I stop and smile?
It will cost me much more to ignore a friend,
Than to help him over a stile.

How much will it cost if I whine and moan,
And long for a magic wand?
BUT, How much will it cost to forget Myself,
And instead hold out my hand?

The Hypnotherapist

I used to drink so heavy,
That I trembled and I shook.
So I went to see this Doctor,
And my last strong drink I took.

But then I started eating,
My body I'd overfeed it.
So I went back to this Doctor,
And he showed me I didn't need it.

But after that I started smoking,
Thirty of forty a day.
And who d'you think it was
That made me throw them all away?

Well, Now my days are filled with SEX,
My nights are utter Bliss.
But no Bloomin' Hypnotherapist
Will stop me having This.

Taken Two Ways

His eyes were kind and gentle,
I felt his presence near,
He led me slowly across the room,
I knew he was sincere.
He laid me down so gently,
His touch was soft and warm,
I could feel his deep eyes studying
my tense and trembling form.
He told me not to worry,
that it would do me good
to let out all my tension,
and in this way I could.
Then his voice was reassuring
(as he sensed my sudden gloom)
that what went on between us
would never leave this room.
He told me now to close my eyes,
to be relaxed and calm,
That he would treat me gently,
and I'd come to no harm.
His soft voice was commanding,
and I did just what he said,
THEN I felt the waves of pleasure,
Like champagne gone to my head.

The moments then that followed
were a mixture of pleasure and pain,
And I seemed to lose all track of time
as I crossed that heavenly plain.
I floated now on a great white cloud,
feelings flowing from within,
And my past flared up before me
as I laid bare everything.
Then I came slowly back to earth,
glowing from head to toe,
I looked into his smiling face,
but no emotion did he show
about the moments we had shared,
You see, there was a twist,
Because I was just his patient,
and he, a Hypnotherapist.

Broken Resolutions

I got my pen and paper,
And looked at the rising Sun.
I wrote down all my resolutions,
'Cause a New Year had begun.

This year I'll do the right thing
With exercise and diet.
I'll have no milk, no eggs, or cheese,
And alcohol, not buy it.

I'll have things that are natural,
'Cause last year I'd gone downhill,
When for all the aches and pains I had,
I just kept taking pills.

And I wouldn't sit in my chair so much,
Thinking I needed rest.
Instead I'd have a walk each day,
And really do my best.

It was such a lovely morning,
"So I'll make a start," I thought.
"And take myself around the block,
For a really good brisk walk."

I started off real slowly,
The air was crisp and cool.
No more would I just sit around,
That was just for fools.

I gradually quickened up my pace,
And was nearly halfway back,
When suddenly something happened
That stopped me in my tracks.

The ground came up to meet me,
And I yelled out in alarm.
Then the pain that shot right through me,
As I landed on my arm.

Later on in Hospital,
(After X-rays and all,
To see that damage I had done
When I had my fall)

The kind and friendly Doctor
Spoke in serious tones,
About my cuts and bruises,
And my broken bones.

Then he looked at me, and smiled and said,
"I know you will be pleased,
'Cause you must sit in a chair and rest
For at least the next six weeks.

And have plenty of milk, and eggs, and cheese,
To help your bones to knit,
And if you feel a bit depressed,
A drink will lift your spirits.

And I'll give you all these pills to take,
To ease your aches and pains,
And if you don't do any exercise
You'll soon be fit again."

Ever Been Ad?

I thought today when for food I went shopping,
I'll buy something nice with my pay,
And by the Adverts they show on the Telly
I know
I'll be sure to save money that way.

In the store on the shelves with the Specials,
All displayed there to catch the keen eye,
I thought, "Isn't that funny,
I've got enough money,
So some of these Bargains I'll buy."

There was the powder they showed on the Telly,
That gets your clothes Whiter than White,
And the paste with a stripe down the middle,
That makes your teeth ever so bright.

"This will last twice as long," said the label
On that washing up liquid so green,
And the stuff that you spray in your Bathroom,
To make the tiles lovely and clean.

Then I came to the shelves with the Goodies,
I thought, "What a tempting display,"
And into me trolley went Chocolate and lollies,
Then I got sort of carried away.

I got Fly spray, and hair spray, and scent spray,
And a bottle of Special Shampoo,
I got Spray for the carpet so the kids wouldn't mark it,
And a blue thing to go down me Loo.

I went mad picking up all the Specials,
Filled me trolley without any fuss,
I thought, "Where would we be without the TV
To make our lives easier for us."

Well, I eventually got to the checkout,
The girl rang it all up then looked black,
'Cause to pay for that stuff, I didn't have nearly enough,
So I had to give half of it back.

I got home from the shops tired and hungry,
With no money, and no food for tea,
'Cause all that I had, was a bloomin' great bagful
Of Specials they showed on TV.

The Diet

"I'll have to go on a diet,"
I told myself today.
"Then all this extra weight I've got,
Will simply go away."

I know I've tried it all before,
Then given up in sorrow,
The many times that I have said,
"I'll start my diet tomorrow."

But this time will be different,
I know that I can do it.
I will just convince myself,
"There's really nothing to it."

So, for breakfast I had Grapefruit,
And half a piece of toast.
For lunch I had a Salad,
While my family ate a Roast.

For dessert I had an Apple,
They had Trifle, Pie and Cream.
My willpower was improving,
The best it's ever been.

I thought, "Dieting is easy,
It's just a piece of CAKE."
Oh dear, I shouldn't have thought that word,
My stomach started to ache.

For tea I had a piece of Cheese,
And Celery, half a stick.
I suddenly thought, "This is Rabbit Food,"
And started to feel sick.

I tried to take my mind off it,
But watching Telly did no good.
'Cause every time the adverts came on,
They just kept showing food.

At last came time to go to bed,
Much more I couldn't take.
But as I tossed and turned about,
I just felt more awake.

So I went down to the kitchen,
To make a cup of tea.
But suddenly something happened,
That took control of me.

I rushed across and opened the fridge,
And staring me in the eye,
Was Trifle, Cream, and cold roast Beef,
And the rest of the Apple Pie.

My knees went weak and trembly,
My stomach was in a knot,
Then before I realised what I'd done,
I sat and scoffed the lot.

I felt so Guilty 'Cause I'd failed,
So to compensate my sorrow,
I made a firm Resolution,
"I'll start my Diet tomorrow."

Sisters

When we were young we used to fight,
And not see eye to eye.
We had an awful lot to learn,
Together, You and I.

But over the years we found out,
What life was all about.
And through it got much closer,
Of that there is no doubt.

We've shared our laughter, Shared our tears,
The good times and the bad.
And I thank Dear God for Sisters,
Mine's the best one to be had.

To A Son

You've given us laughter,
You've given us tears.
You've given us hopes,
You've given us fears.

We've shared in your Problems,
We've shared in your Dreams.
We've shared in your Heartaches,
We've shared in your Schemes.

We've shared, And we've given,
What came from above.
And that Was, and Will be
Our undying Love.

A Card to the One I Love

You may wonder why I've sent you this card,
Well to give you the reason is not very hard.

It isn't your Birthday, or Christmas my dear,
And it's not 'cause our Anniversary is here.

You've not had a baby, or just passed your Test,
It's not a Get Well card, Your health's at its best.

It's not Bon Voyage, you're not going to roam,
You've not been away, So it's not Welcome Home.

So you may well ask why I've sent you this card,
Well, to give you the reason is not very hard.

It's just a little something you see, to say
"THANK YOU MY DARLING for JUST LOVING ME."

The Change in Me

Last week I went to see the Doctor,
'Cause I'd been feeling pretty queer.
He smiled in his usual friendly way,
And said, "What's up my dear?"
So I told him that just lately
Things was 'appening to me,
And I just wasn't the woman
That I used to be.
I told him I 'ad feelings
Of creepy crawly things,
And pins and needles in me 'ands,
And bad imaginings.
I told him I kept going 'ot,
Especially in me face.
I'd get fluttery feelings in me chest,
Then me 'eart would start to race.
And sometimes I'd get all tensed up
For no reason at all.
Then I'd get bouts of bad depression
That I just could not control.

I told him I felt bloated,
I was putting on the weight.
Sometimes I'd get the trembles,
I'd even get the shakes.
And my family couldn't understand it
When I didn't feel too good,
And was much too tired to do the things
I knew I really should.
Yet I said at night I couldn't sleep,
I'd lay for hours in bed.
And all the aches and pains I 'ad,
And funny feelings in me 'ead.
Well, the doctor smiled kindly,
And he said, "Don't look so sad."
Then he reassured me
That I wasn't going mad.
He'd patiently sat and listened
to my problems, what a range.
Then he smiled and said, "Don't worry dear,
You're just going through the CHANGE."

Puppy Love

I wandered down the High Street,
Feeling lonely as could be.
If only I had a little friend
To keep me company.
Then I saw him in a window,
Looking so forlorn.
But he wagged his tail when he saw me,
And his eyes said, "Please take me home.
I'll be your very Special friend,
And I'll love you, O so true."
That little Pup in the window,
With eyes so very Blue.
I paid the man and I took him,
His grateful eyes did shine.
At last we'd found each other,
And I had a friend all mine.
I taught him lots of clever tricks,
And he'd romp around the place.
He was so soft and friendly,
And he'd lick me on my face.
We'd go for walks, he'd stay by me,
As if as much to say.
"I love you very dearly,
And I'll never go away."
I had him for a long, long time,
We never were apart.
He was my very Special friend,
Whom I loved with all my heart.

One day I heard the screech of brakes,
Not giving a second thought,
Until I went outside and saw
My little friend was caught
Beneath the wheels of a big black car,
He lay so very still,
The little one I loved so much,
Taken from me. Till
I realised I'd lost my friend,
Whatever would I do?
I'd never see those eyes again,
Saying, "I Love You."

A long time passed before I thought
Things would ever be the same.
Then I found myself wandering
Down the High Street once again.
I expected to see an empty box
In that window I'd looked before,
But instead I saw two little Brown eyes,
And the rise of a tiny paw.
He looked at me so loving,
And my heart just started to roam
Back to the eyes that had said before,
"Please will you take me home?"
It was happening again, as it happened then,
And I thought, "My heart won't mend."
So I walked away . . . But then turned back,
Everyone needs a friend.

To Our First Born

You may have often wondered
Over the passing years,
Why we've given so much love to you,
Through laughter and through tears.
But soon you'll know the reason
Why sometimes we've made a fuss.
Why we've always wanted the best for you,
Why you mean so much to us.
It doesn't seem so long ago
We held you in our arms.
A tiny gift from Heaven above,
Full of endearing charms.
And we marvelled at the miracle
Of what Dear God had done,
In making a perfect baby for us,
Your Dad and Mum.
We remember with joy your very first smile,
And the first words that you said,
And how we'd creep in and watch you,
When you were asleep in bed.
How you learnt to walk, and talk and play,
Always something new.
And we thanked God for the Wonderful gift
He'd given us, in you.
Soon your baby days were over,
And with each passing mile
We taught you everything we knew
To make your life worthwhile.

How we laughed when you were happy,
And cried when you were sad.
How we cared for you when you were sick,
When you were better, we were glad.
We remember oh so many things,
And as the years have passed,
All those little things will stay with us
As memories that will last.
Now very soon it will happen again,
We'll live those days anew.
As God will give a child again,
But this time He'll give it to You.
And You'll marvel at the Miracle
As you hold it in your arms.
That tiny gift from Heaven above,
Full of endearing charms.
And it's THEN you'll know, just how WE felt,
And WHY all the love we've shown.
Because you'll realise just what it means,
To have a child of your own.

The Hysterectomy or the Root of the Trouble

I struggled into Hospital
The best way that I could.
'Cause I had this awful belly ache,
And I didn't feel too good.

Well, they pulled me this way, They pulled me that,
They had a good look round,
As far inside as they could see,
And suddenly they found

A little thing they call the womb,
That was making me so sore.
So they put me under, and took it out,
My ovaries and all.

It wasn't a pleasant experience
To go through all that pain,
And have that interference,
I thought I'd never be the same.

But I've been told by one who knows,
That 'cause of that interference,
Now, as far as my love life goes,
It won't make a bit of difference.

In fact it should be better
Now I've had my Hysterection.
'Cause there's no chance of Copping Out,
When my Man gets An Erection.

A Mother's Prayer

You must get many prayers, dear God,
That take up all your time,
But I hope some way or other
you'll hear, and answer mine.
I always say a prayer, dear God
to you, when things go wrong,
Please help me in my weaknesses,
Please help me be more strong.
Please give me confidence every day,
To do the things I should,
For my Husband and my family,
And help me to be good.
Please see my children through their ills,
And dry up any tears,
Always please be with them,
And see them through their years.
And when they have to leave the nest,
And go their separate ways,
Please help them, guide them, keep them safe,
Don't let them go astray.
But if they should get bad times,
Please teach them how to smile,
Just give them all the strength to know
that life is still worthwhile.
You must get many prayers, Dear God,
That take up all your time,
But I know someway or other
you'll hear, and answer mine,
Because, Dear God, you always have,
To help these lives we live,
And if sometimes I forget to thank you,
Dear God up above, Please forgive.

Never Date a Doctor

Some women fall in love with their Doctors,
And that is very true.
But ladies you might change your minds,
When this story I've told you.
One day I met this smashing man,
Oh I felt so very proud,
'Cause he told me he was a Doctor,
And would like to take me out.
Well, We had a lovely night,
Then we went back to his place.
The thought of a Doctor making love
Made the blood rush to my face.
Well, He took my trembling hand in his,
But then I thought, "How False."
'Cause instead of offering me a drink,
He started to take my pulse.
Then he very gently caressed my neck,
Oh he had such lovely hands.
But then he pressed it hard and said,
"You've got swollen glands."
Then he moved his hand down to my breast,
But I felt a proper chump.
'Cause instead of whispering tender words,
He said, "You've got a lump."
Then his hands went lower to my stomach,
But I wanted to shout.

'Cause he just pressed it hard and said,
"That appendix will have to come out."
Then he ran his hands all down my legs,
From the top down to my toes.
But all he said was, "Hm, varicose veins,
We'll have to get rid of those."
Then he put his hand upon my knee,
And I thought, "Oh Heaven help us,"
But D'you know what he said to me?
He said, "You've got Arthritis."
THEN he went up higher,
And my blood just started to rush.
But he just took one look and said,
"Do you know you've got THRUSH?"
Then he said he'd like to get me in bed,
But my happiness turned to sorrow.
'Cause he said,
"There's some vacant in the Hospital,
And I'll book you in tomorrow."
I thought, "Right mate, That does it,"
And I think I've learned me lesson,
If I ever date a man again,
I'll make sure he's not in That Profession.

The Boil - As told by a young man

I came round in the recovery room
Feeling sick and very sore,
But I suppose I should expect that,
When they'd just removed a Boil.

Any other time I wouldn't mind,
But now I was full of gloom,
'Cause this boil had come up on my "You know what"
The first night of our Honeymoon.

We'd waited so long for our Wedding day,
And the night to end all nights.
When I'd prove at last I was a man,
But now I was in this plight.

She said she wanted lots of Kids,
They were nice to have around,
And I'd promised her I'd do my bit,
And I wouldn't let her down.

I looked over at the bloke laid next to me,
God, why did he look so well,
After the operation he'd just had,
He should have been going through Hell.

I'd met him before we had our Op's,
And he'd said, "KIDS" he wanted no more,
But his wife had refused to take the Pill,
So I knew what he'd come in for.

I thought, "The Silly Bugger,"
He must be round the Bend,
My Producing days would soon begin,
But his had come to an end.

Then they wheeled us back into the ward,
I felt I could hardly move,
But soon I'd be back with my lovely Bride,
And my Manhood I would prove.

Later on the Doctor came around,
And he examined the bloke next door,
Then a Funny look came over his face,
What it meant I wasn't sure.

Till he raced around to my bed,
And what followed I just couldn't take,
As he quickly pulled back the sheets and said,
"Oh MY God, . . . We've made a mistake."

My Special Place

Whenever life gets hectic,
And thoughts race through my mind,
I find myself a quiet spot
where I can just unwind.
I close my eyes, then start to drift
way back in time and space,
And find myself just once again
in a very Special Place.
A place I know from long ago,
In a land so fair and green,
Where everything was peaceful,
A place where I could dream.
I wander through a leafy glade,
Where trees are tall and strong,
And from their branches up above,
The birds are full of song.
I gradually feel myself unwind,
My breathing starts to slow,
And a quiet peace drifts over me,
in this place of long ago.
Then I come across a little stream,
Over stones the waters fall,
And I am filled with wonder
at the beauty of it all.
Around me I see cottages,
With gardens full of flowers,
Their fragrance fills my nostrils,
As I gaze at every bower.

I see old men leaning on the fence,
Just passing the time of day,
They look up and smile, and wave at me
In a very friendly way.
The sky is blue, the sun is warm,
contentment fills my mind,
And in this very Special Place
Tranquillity I find.
Then from deep inside me
A quiet voice I hear,
That speaks to me and gives me strength
And drives out all my fears.
My energies are recharging
with all these sights and sounds,
There is peace and relaxation,
And calmness all around.
I stay a while, then soon I drift
again through time and space,
Back to this life that rushes by
at such a hectic place.
But I know (in my Mind) at any time
to my Haven I can go,
With those trees and birds,
That stream and flowers,
My place of long ago,
And I know that it will fill me
with such Tranquillity,
That when I return to here and now,
I will be rested, and feel Free.

Greetings

To buy a card, you go into the store,
And see them displayed, a thousand or more.
You really find it quite amazing,
They have a card for every occasion.
They've got children's cards for every age,
And ones with a verse on every page.
There's Anniversary, Birthday, and all the rest,
Like Congratulations on passing your Test.
They've got cards for Sweetheart to show you care,
And look at those funny ones over there.
There are cards for Father, and Daughter, and Son,
And the ones for Mother are second to none.
They've got ones with flowers, and animals too,
And trees and birds, to name just a few.
They've got ones with boats, and lakes, and trees,
You're sure to find a card to please.
There are Sympathy, Get Well, and Bon Voyage,
Some very tine, some very large.
Whatever you want they've got them all,
Ones for Brother and Sister, Even Mother-in-Law.
You have such a job to make your selection,
The way they're displayed is just perfection.
You ought to go and be on your way,
But you just can't leave this lovely display.
You only came in for just One card,
But there are so many, You find it hard
To buy just one, They are all so good,
That you end up buying more than you should.

To Eric

You speak such words of wisdom,
Just like the three wise men.
You find, and help the lost sheep,
Like the shepherds in Bethlehem.
You're gentle, like the Mother
Who in her arms did cradle that child.
You're like the Guardian Angel,
Who watched over the stable.
God sent out all these people,
To see that infant through,
Then he took a part of each of them,
And created You.

Angels

(To Dorothy)

Some people think of Angels
As wearing white with wings.
Some people think of them as
Little choirboys that sing.
Some people think of Angels
As floating from heaven above.
Some think of little cupids,
Who shoot their arrows of love.
The definitions of an Angel
Are all different, it is true.
But when I think of an Angel,
I Always think of you.

Just For today

I'll take the time each morning
To quietly sit and pray,
That God will help me follow this guide
below, JUST FOR TODAY.

I'll try to live this day alone,
The best way that I can,
'Cause to keep it up for a lifetime
would appal me, as I am.
Today I will be happy,
As Abe Lincoln said to me,
That folks are only as happy,
As they make up their minds to be.
Today I will try to strengthen my mind,
I will study and learn something new.
I will not be a mental loafer,
I'll make the effort, and concentrate too.
I will do somebody a good turn,
But I won't get found out,
'Cause if anybody knows of it,
It really will not count.
I will do at least two things
That I don't want to do,
And if I'm hurt, not show it,
Though I may be hurt it's true.

Today I'll dress becomingly,
Act Courteous, and talk low,
Be agreeable, not criticise one bit,
The best in me I'll show.
I'll not find fault with anything,
Not crave for power or wealth,
Not try to improve or regulate
Anybody, but myself.
Today I'll have a program,
To follow it I'll try,
And from hurry and indecision,
To save myself will I.
Today for half an hour,
I'll relax and be alone.
Get a better perspective of my life,
And pray that I'll be shown.
Today I will be unafraid
Of the beautiful things I see,
And believe that as I give to the world,
So the world will give to me.

That Special Smile

The church is full of people,
And I see you standing there,
Waiting for the girl to come
Who's life you soon will share.
I try so hard to stop the tears
that I feel begin to flow,
As you stand there with your back to me,
I wonder if you know
How much I've always loved you,
Right from the very start,
The first time that I saw you
I'd given you my heart.
You always had a Special Smile
that I knew was just for me,
And you'd hug me oh so tight
for all the world to see.
Oh I think of the many times,
(So easy to recall)
When you'd given me that smile,
And said you loved me Best of all.
And now you're getting married
to a girl you hardly know,
But you told me she was the one for you,
So I will let you go.
Now I think of the Happy times we shared,
Always side by side,
And if I used to get upset,
How you'd hug me when I cried,
Then later on when you went away,
(And I was on my own)
You wrote me a letter Every day,

And when you came back home
you brought me a bunch of flowers,
The biggest I'd ever seen,
And you gave me that Special Smile,
And said I'd always be your Queen.
Now this church is Full of flowers,
And your eyes are full of pride,
As you turn and look back down the aisle
to see your lovely bride.
She comes to stand beside you,
The church is quiet and still,
I hear you make your promises,
I hear you say "I Will."
Now it seems I've really lost you,
And I fight the tears in vain,
All those years we had together,
We'll never have again.
And now the wedding's over,
BUT, as you walk back down the aisle
you stop by me, and hug me,
And give me that Special Smile.
And all at once I'm happy,
And all my tears are gone,
Because Suddenly I realise,
You'll Always be . . . MY SON.

The Empty Nest

When all my kids got married,
And moved away from home,
I thought, "Whatever can I do,
Now I am on my own?"

I'd been so busy all those years,
With all there was to do,
Like cooking, washing, cleaning,
The things all Mothers do.

But now at last the time had come,
When my chicks had left the nest.
So I'd have to get a Hobby,
And see what I did best.

First of all I took up knitting,
But that really was a flop,
'Cause the jumper that I started,
Turned out to be a sock.

So I tried my hand at Crochet,
To satisfy my soul,
But all I ended up with
Was a big square full of holes.

Perhaps Macrame was the answer,
But my spirits soon did flag,
'Cause my lovely hanging basket
Ended up as a string bag.

So I thought I'd take up swimming,
But I felt a proper fool,
'Cause with my weight I kept sinking
To the bottom of the pool.

Then I thought I'd take up Jogging,
But that nearly was my death,
'Cause after running halfway round the block,
I just ran out of breath.

Then I thought I'd learn to drive the car,
But I was a bag of nerves,
'Cause instead of going forward,
I kept going in reverse.

By the time I'd tried out all these things,
I was a total wreck,
So to relax I took up Yoga,
But got me legs stuck round me neck.

Then very soon my children,
Had children of their own,
So at last I found the answer,
Doing what I'd always done.

'Cause now I just look after them,
And that really suits me fine,
So for all those little Hobbies,
I just don't have the time.

Celebrating Christmas

Christmas comes but once a year,
And when it comes it brings good cheer.
But do we think when we're Merry and gay,
Just WHY we celebrate Christmas Day?

We've been so busy the weeks before,
Preparing and doing all those chores,
Like rushing around buying presents and food,
Getting all tired and not feeling good.

Putting up trimmings, and tinsel and lights,
Rearranging the tree to get it just right.
Sending out cards, there's always a lot,
Then buying more for those we forgot.

Break-up parties with plenty of drink,
Some get all stupid because they don't think.
People driving their cars with undue care,
As if they've not got a minute to spare.

Children excited, just counting the days,
To see what Santa brings on his sleigh.
Cleaning the house through as though it's a sin
To have it untidy if people drop in.

Last minute shopping to buy extra stuff,
Just in case we've not got enough.
And when the day comes we're all worn out,
Wondering what it's all about.

But it will be a time well spent,
If we Really celebrate the Event
That happened on that Christmas Day,
Long ago, and Far away.

In the lowly surroundings of a cattle stall,
Where a child was born to save us all.

So when that Special Day arrives,
Let us pause, and look to the skies.
And remember,
When everyone's getting merry and gay,
Just WHY we celebrate Christmas Day.

God's Gift

When GOD created you for us,
He had one thing in mind.
To make a lovely Daughter,
Of a Special kind.

He picked out the ingredients
From everything he knew,
Like the colours of the rainbow,
And the early morning dew.

He took a ray of sunshine,
And from the sky above,
He picked a very Special star,
And sprinkled it with love.

He took a sprig of laughter,
And added than a tear.
A petal from a fragrant Rose,
Some Crystal pure and clear.

God gathered many precious things,
And when his task was through,
He moulded them together,
And Created You.

In Charge

I only seem to pray to you
Dear Lord, when things go wrong,
When my load is heavy,
And my heart has lost its song.

When troubles just keep crowding in,
And I can't find the way
Out of all my problems,
Then is the time I pray.

But other times I manage,
When things are going good,
And I forget to talk to you,
The way I know I should.

It's then I do things My way,
And try to run the show,
Forgetting YOU have shown me
Everything I know.

It's then I feel so very sure
That I am in control,
That I know all the answers,
That I can save the souls.

So DEAR LORD keep reminding me
That I can't run the show,
Let me only see that YOU
have taught me all I know.

Let me pray when things go RIGHT,
Teach me LORD to see,
That I am not the one in charge,
But YOU are in charge of me.

To A Daughter From Her Mum

When you were very small,
And your troubles I helped you through,
In your own little way you thanked me,
But you never said, "Mum, I love you."

Then as the years went by,
And into a girl you grew,
I watched you with such pride and joy,
But you never said, "Mum, I love you."

Your teenage years were lovely,
You bought me presents, and helped me too.
But I'd have gone without all those things,
If you'd only said "Mum, I love you."

I never knew Why you couldn't say it,
It would have meant more than a smile,
Those little words that I longed to hear,
To make it all worthwhile.

Then you fell in love, and got married,
And I thought Then you might come through.
Instead of "Thanks, Mum, for everything,"
You could just say, "Mum, I love You."

Very soon you had a daughter,
A little one of your own.
And you'll care for her as I cared for you,
And you will watch Her grow.

Today you came to see me,
You stood there and held out your hand.
You suddenly looked different,
You seemed to understand.

Then you put your arms around me,
And said, "Dear Mum, I LOVE YOU."
And I knew Why at last you could say it,
Because now, You're a Mother Too.

Letting Go . . . (Of a Daughter or Son)

When my Son decided to leave us,
And branch out on his own,
I couldn't understand Why
He should want to leave his home.

All the years that I had guided him,
Through what he had to do.
I'd listened to his problems,
And always helped him through.

I'd lent him money when he was broke,
Though seldom got it back.
But I did things with a willing heart,
My love he didn't lack.

Now suddenly I was cast off,
Not needed any more.
And I started to think all sorts of things,
Felt hurt, and sad, and sore.

Who will do his washing?
And make sure that he is fed?
What if he is cold and tired,
And hasn't got a bed?

Who'll be there to care for him
If he is suddenly ill?
Where will he find the money
To pay unwanted bills?

What if he gets in bad company?
And into wilful ways?
What if someone hurts him,
And he cannot get away?

Who'll listen to his problems,
And help him through his fears?
Who will hold him in their arms,
And wipe away his tears?

He won't have my protection,
Or cope if I'm not there.
However will he manage,
Without his Mother's care?

Then the words, "Let Go and Let God"
Suddenly came to me.
If only I knew how to do that!
From my worrying, I'd be Free.

So slowly I have had to learn
That I must just Let Go,
And leave the only One above who cares,
To run the show.

Just pray, "Dear God, Take care of him,
Protect him from all harm."
Then Trust that HE will keep him safe,
In His everlasting Arms.

Mine For A Day

I have my precious child every week,
To look after for a day.
If only it was for always,
And they didn't take him away.

But the Law says I cannot keep him,
He is not mine to be had.
But he can be with me now and then,
And for that I'm very glad.

I still love his Father very much,
But it wasn't meant to be,
For us to stay together,
So I had to set him free.

He now belongs to another,
Together they're raising this child,
And they're making a really good job of it,
So I mustn't be jealous or wild.

But just for today this boy is mine,
To keep in my loving care.
I'll forget he has to leave me again,
Every precious moment we'll share.

I make the most of the time with him,
On these very Special days.
I tell him stories, We read and draw,
Or go to the park and play.

Sometimes he falls and hurts his knee,
And his tears I have to dry.
God, He's so much like his Father,
When he looks at me with those eyes.

Then he gets tired and I lay him down,
So beautiful as he sleeps.
And my heart overflows with love for him,
I wish I had him to keep.

But soon they'll come to take him back,
Once again I'll be alone.
Just waiting for the next time,
This child is allowed to come.

Then when they arrive to pick him up,
He hugs me, and kisses my cheek.
And as they drive away he waves,
Calling out,
"Bye Grandma . . . See you next week."

The Three Wise Monkeys and Me

Four wise monkeys sat in a tree,
Called SEENO, HEARNO, SPEAKNO, and ME.
They all have advice to help you make it,
And your life will be happy if you take it.
The first one tells you, "If you're wise,
Against all evil you'll close your eyes."
The second one tells you, "If you can,
Hear no evil of any man."
"Speak no evil and always be true."
That's what the third monkey's telling you.
"These three wise monkeys are very good,
And to take their advice I think you should,"
Says the fourth little monkey sat in the tree,
The one on the end, that I said was me,
Giving the wisest advice of all,
"Just do your best, and you'll stand tall."

Dear God

To accept the things I cannot change,
SERENITY please give,
The COURAGE to change the things I can,
A better life to live.
Then Dear Father up above,
I really pray to you,
To give me the WISDOM that I may know,
The difference between the two.

My Special Day

Today's a very Special Day
That I've looked forward to.
I got up nice and early,
There is so much to do.

I've had a shower, washed my hair,
I really must look nice.
The time is going much too slow,
I check it once or twice.

I wash the dishes, mop the floor,
To pass the time away,
I check again, it won't be long
Till I am on my way.

I open up the wardrobe,
Get out my Special dress,
Then put on my new white shoes,
I want to look my best.

I'm getting so excited,
I really cannot wait.
I look out of the window,
I hope the car's not late.

Then it arrives, my friends are here,
All calling out the lingo.
I leave the house,
Get into the car.
Hurray, we're off to Bingo.

That First Drink

The next time I get the urge to drink,
I will stop, and I will think,
"It's just a habit I've got into,
But habits are hard to break, it's true.
If I do something else, and that FIRST DRINK delay,
In time the craving will go away."
BUT. . . If to the lips I put even a fraction,
It will start off a chain reaction.
Just one drop of that sweet stuff
inside me will be enough . . . to start me off.
Then later on I will think,
"It won't hurt to have another drink,
And if I just have a little drop,
I know that I can always stop.
Because let's face it after all,
I know that I am in control."

GOD, Who am I fooling, only myself,
'Cause as long as that drink is on the shelf,
Or in the Wardrobe hidden away,
I know I'll drink the lot today.

And so it goes on as I try to hide
All that I'm drinking on the side.
And the ones I love will all act FORMAL,
As I try very hard to just act NORMAL,
Although my eyes are rather blurred,
And my speech is rather slurred.

Later on I'll need to sleep,
I'll just drop down and go so deep,
But not for long. It always seems
I'm troubled by those restless dreams.
Then when morning comes I'll want to stay
Where I am with the world far away.
The troubles I thought I had, and cares,
Will seem much more of a burden to bear.

Then the Guilt will set in, the Depression, Remorse,
As it always does of course.
And as long as onto that bottle I hold,
I'll always feel left out in the cold.

BUT, Some think I'm Special and really worth saving,
If only I could stop when I get that craving,
Because It's only a habit I got into,
And Habits CAN be broken it's true.
But if to my lips I put even a fraction,
It will start off that chain reaction.
Just ONE DROP of that sweet stuff
Inside of me will be enough.

So the next time I get the urge to drink,
I WILL STOP, and I will think,
"If I do something else, and the FIRST DRINK delay,
If I pick up the phone & ring 'AA'
With their help the Craving Will go away.

Fagged Out

When I was young I took up smoking,
It seemed the thing to do.
But if I'd never started,
I'd still be here it's true.
I didn't smoke too many,
Just one now and then.
But one day when I counted up,
I realised I'd had ten.
Then it got to be a habit,
And I got a nagging cough.
But when I tried to give it up,
I found I couldn't stop.
To the warning on the packet
I really paid no heed.
I'd just open up the packet,
And light up another weed.
To get up in the mornings,
became an awful drag.
And as soon as I got out of bed,
I'd have to have a fag.
I wouldn't go on a train or bus,
I'd always drive the car.
So I could fill me lungs with smoke,
And nicotine and tar.
When I went to the pictures,
It really was no joke,
Cause I'd spend half me time outside,
Just having another smoke.
I used to watch those films on lungs,
But really couldn't see
That what happened to people who smoke a lot
Could really happen to me.

Mind you, sometimes when I lit one up,
It would give me quite a scare,
'Cause when I went to use the ashtray,
I'd have another one burning there.
And to smoke in bed was dangerous,
As I very soon found out.
'Cause when I woke up the fire brigade
Was putting the fire out.
Then I really tried to give it up,
But I thought I'd go insane.
And after half and hour
I just lit up again.
Then I got a bad pain in me chest,
"Slow down" it seemed to say.
But I just lit up another fag,
And hoped it would go away.
The Doctor told me to give it up,
But to smoking I was a slave.
I thought, "The only time I'll give it up
Is when I'm in me grave."

When they laid me in me coffin,
There were no flowers in my hand,
Just a little box of matches,
And a packet of me favourite brand.

And on me headstone when they buried me,
The words were very clear,
IF SHE'D ONLY GIVEN UP SMOKING,
SHE WOULD SURELY STILL BE HERE.

The Garage Sale

I'd hoarded a lot of things over the years
That were just collecting dust.
So I thought I'd have a GARAGE SALE,
And get rid of some of this stuff.
I really could make some money,
If some of these things I sold.
'Cause let's face it I never use them,
And most of them are old.
I've got boxes, and cupboards, and wardrobes,
That are full up to the brim.
If I cleared a lot of it out,
I could put some more stuff in.
There are vases, plates and ornaments,
And Tupperware with no lids.
There are all my children's books and toys
That I've kept since they were kids.
There's that china in my cupboard,
A present from Aunty Jean.
But it's been in the family for years,
So to sell it would be a bit mean.
There are clothes and shoes in my wardrobe,
That are really out of date.
But they might come back into fashion,
So perhaps I'd better wait.
The sewing machine was my Mother's.
I can't give that away.
No I think I'd better hang on to that.
It might be worth something one day.
And all my long playing records,
That I've had since way back then.
They might be collectors items,
So I'd better hang on to them.

There's all that lovely jewelry
That I never wear.
But each piece was a present from someone,
So to sell them wouldn't be fair.
I've got boxes of books and magazines,
That I look at now and then.
I'd better hang on to those,
I might want to read them again.
All this stuff that I've collected,
I might use again, who can tell.
So I think I'd better give up the idea
Of having a GARAGE SALE.

The Recipe

Take a cup of kindness,
A measure of good cheer.
Add a heap of sympathy,
Some laughter and a tear.
Then some understanding,
Compassion and a smile.
Mix them altogether,
Then let it stand awhile.
After that add humour,
Some faith from up above,
And remember always,
To add undying love.
Mix up these ingredients,
And when the job is done.
You'll have the perfect mixture,
That makes a perfect Mum.

The Monster

Last night I had an awful dream
That I was at the Zoo.
Being chased by tigers,
Giraffes and Rhinos too.

I tried so hard to get away,
But every path I took,
Dolphins leaped in front of me,
And Pirates with their hooks.

Funny birds flew overhead,
And as I looked around
There were alligators, Dinosaurs,
And snakes upon the ground.

Then a monster loomed in front of me,
Which wasn't very funny,
'Cause it kept playing a silly tune,
And gobbled up my money.

This monster had me in its grip,
Much more I couldn't take.
Each time I tried to get away,
I just could not escape.

I woke up with an awful scream,
And that is where the joke is.
I realised why I'd had that dream,
'Cause I'm addicted to the Pokies.

Disciples

A long time ago in Bethlehem,
Jesus Christ was born,
To save the lives of sinners,
The downcast and forlorn.

He picked out twelve Disciples,
Just simple fishermen,
To help him in his task of Peace,
And Goodwill to all men.

That was oh so long ago,
But his task was carried on,
And today he has millions of Disciples,
And I thank Jesus Christ I've met some.

Memories

(to Pat)

I'd love to turn the clock back
To the days of long ago.
To a time when life was peaceful,
And the pace was nice and slow.

When we didn't have the Telly,
With all the stupid ad's,
But listened to the wireless,
And sat in with Mum and Dad.

When films were so romantic,
The hero took our breath away.
When love was soft and gentle,
Not the sex they show today.

When dancing was a pleasure,
And picnics by the lake.
When we poured tea from a teapot,
And had biscuits on a plate.

Although I cannot turn the clock back,
There is one thing that I know.
I'll always have my Memories
Of those days of long ago.

Goodbye Mum

Dear Mum you were a person
Quite apart from all the rest,
You gave your never ending Love,
You did your very Best.

You listened to our problems,
And all our joys you shared,
And any time we needed you,
We always found you there.

Always there to lend a hand
In everything we'd do,
You'd help us, Guide us, Comfort us,
With a love that was so true.

We took so much for Granted,
And though we tried to show we cared,
We've only realised your Value,
Now we find that you're not there.

So when you look down on us,
And you ask the reason Why
You see how much we're hurting,
And you see how much we cry,

Well, It's Just because we love you,
And it's SO HARD to let go
Of the Dearest, and the Kindest,
Precious Mum we'll ever know.

The End

Well, I' hope you liked my poems,
And maybe had a laugh.
Or perhaps a little tear
At some memory of the past.
'Cause let's face it we're all Women
With feelings, Oh so true.
And where would the world be without us,
People like Me and You.